Paleo Diet Recipes for Beginners

Boost Your Health and Feel Great with These Easy and Delicious Recipes to Cook at Home on a Budget

Elisa Williams

TABLE OF CONTENTS

Introduction to Paleo Diet

A paleo diet food list is that the ideal diet that depends on the dietary requirements set up all through the transformative way to the current sort for the human creatures - having the natural name of Homo sapiens. Paleo diet is moreover known as the naturally worthy diet. The stylish dietary routine is alluded to as the Paleo diet food list shortened as a Paleo diet or paleo diet, which is also prominently called the caveman diet, tracker assembled diet, or Stone Age diet. Paleo food of that period comprised wild plants and wild creatures devoured by the men of the said time. Paleolithic age finished with the advancement of ongoing horticultural procedures and thoughts around 10,000 years prior. The subject behind the idea about the practicality of the Paleolithic diet for humans is that the legitimate diet for human well-being ought to be intently like the genealogical diet. A Paleo diet food rundown ought to be made out of them on top of referenced fixings. Starting with the meat, that ought to be eaten as a ton of joined will however the reason to recall is that the meat should be cooked basic without adding a great deal of the fats because fats cause a few infections like pulse, cholesterol and increment the odds of deadly respiratory failure by obstructing the section of blood flow. By remembering this time, meat is solid for us whether we use it inside the morning meal, lunch, or supper. Lean beef is the beef managed of noticeable fats, and the lean meats rundown can be extended to contain the lean hamburger, flank steak, extra-lean burger, lean veal, Chunk steak, London cooks, Top sirloin steak, and any unique slim cut. Lean poultry comprises chicken bosom, turkey bosom, and game hen bosom having chicken with skin eliminated. Eggs at most extreme six in seven days of duck, goose, and chicken (select the enhanced Omega 3 choice of chicken eggs).

Elective sorts of meat may fuse bunny and goat meat. Game meat should comprise crocodile, bear, buffalo or bison, kangaroo, and so forth. Fish meat is likewise ideal to be utilized as a diet. The meat inside the Paleo diet food list comes to the number of products of the soil vegetables. A few people believe that products of the soil increment the weight and make them fat. Comparable to the higher than, this can be unmistakably the main misguided judgment regarding the incorporation of organic products inside the way of life. Natural products don't expand the load at all, paying little mind to how bountiful you eat it as leafy foods vegetables contains extremely low measures of calories. For the ideal life and well-being, every dinner should exemplify a mix of meat, salad, vegetables, nuts, seeds, and natural products like apples, pomegranates, grapes, apricots, figs, and bananas in his diet. Oranges, lemon, pears, pineapples, watermelons, and Papaya are among the renowned natural products because they contain higher water measure and subsequently give additional energy to the benefactor. As to different foodstuffs remembered for the Paleo diet, in an episode of effectively getting more fit, at the most extreme, four ounces of nuts and seeds ought to be utilized. Pecans are among the easiest because they contain the most significant proportion of Omega 3. Oils, drinks, and Paleo desserts should conjointly be utilized in moderate amounts. Furthermore, recollect that Paleo diet food rundown won't contain everything handled foods made out of a dairy item, powdered milk, frozen yogurts, oat grains, and vegetables and should be kept away from. The overall low-carb diets shun eating any carbs while the Paleo Diet nuts and bolts epitomize things like new foods grown from the ground.

The Paleo Diet also doesn't accept any dairy that might be a major dietary disadvantage for a few groups. Such a large number of long stretches of chemical-bound milk has made even people who should endure dairy well touchy or even oversensitive to it. The Paleo Diet incredibly centers around more modest pieces of upper-quality supplements by definition. The Paleo diet, likewise called the Paleolithic Diet, could be a dietary arrangement that is predicated on the assumed diet of our progenitors living inside the Paleolithic period. Such cases are as yet discussed these days by specialists and well-being experts. Indeed, even consequently, since the renewed introduction of this diet mastermind, it has been considered by a few in show effective arrangement accomplish a better life. The prior arrangement of the Paleo diet plan is to burn through foods that are eatable in their normal state or the event that it does might want to be cooked. It should be, at any rate, set up in the best methods feasible. It is designed by the way of life of our predecessors who survived demonstrations of looking, fishing, and assembling edible plants. The accommodation of cooking wasn't out there around then.

I amazingly like concerning this diet because I just

fundamentally need to bring up a practical issue after thinking about a portion of certain food. If I was living in the Stone age, would this food be offered to me? It's eye-catching to consider that while the people of that day neglected to have the innovation or the indistinguishable abundance of food that we tend to savor these days, that they, in a real sense, we're in a situation to deliver their bodies with more characteristic foods and supplements in each meat that they ate. People searching for a good dieting plan might be overpowered by the number of choices for dinner designs out there. The Paleo diet or caveman diet takes its motivation from the human tribal air itself, at least reliable with our speculations worried that point sum. People in the familial setting didn't eat stylishly prepared foods. Anyway, they might not have eaten any of the foods that we will, in general, presently accompany an agricultural way of life. Dairy products, bread, and grain stock are farming in nature. This diet is tied in with returning to our underlying foundations to an enormous degree, subsequently to talk. This diet fuses various distinctive dietary standards. There has been a generous amount of discussion over the years on whether individuals should lessen their admission of fats or starches. The contention gets even extra confounded when people bring up whether it's a straightforward matter of practicing good eating habits, fats, and sound cards and keeping away from their undesirable partners. Paleo comes out rigorously on the discussion that favors fats over sugars. However, it will, in general, accentuate monounsaturated fats instead of immersed fats.

The Paleo diet puts an exacting weight on eating the lean cuts of meat. In general, this diet is low in sugars. People eating the ordinary Western diet will get the vast majority of their sugars from bread and improved drinks. On the Paleo diet, the vast majority of your carbs can return from leafy foods, which are normally low in calories and accordingly contain relatively a couple of carbs. In a nutshell, people on the Paleo will burn through meat, natural products, vegetables, and nuts, oils, and flavors. Dairy items and grain items are off the menu. There is a significant measure of a continuous conversation concerning the general advantages of the Paleo diet. Anyway, some qualities will well advance well-being by their own doing. For a certain something, individuals can understand themselves devouring not very many undesirable prepared foods while on the Paleo diet, and handled foods can be loaded down with unfortunate and untested food added substances. A few nutritionists and dieticians concur that refined sugar is unfortunate, and individuals will acknowledge eating pretty much zero teaspoons of refined sugar while on this diet. While numerous other low-starch diets tend to be too high in unfortunate fats, the Paleo places an exceptional weight on nuts and seeds' fats, which numerous dieticians and nutritionists recommend modestly.

Though the basic study of the Paleo diet is continually under examination, a few of its key standards appear to be founded on sound dietary hypothesis. A few groups beginning Paleo could see it depleting to deal with at first. For certain people, it may address a stunning dietary change. People may wind up cooking extra regularly to get ready delicious Paleo recipes. The developing prevalence of the Paleo diet should help make progress simpler for people curious about improving their well-being. Regularly known as the caveman diet because of its reference to being a Stone Age diet, the Paleo Diet is nothing extra than eating foods that are, for the most part, common. For instance, the sorts of foods that are considered satisfactory in this diet can be individuals who might be out there all through the Stone Age time. It would comprise wild plants, nuts, vegetables, meat, fish, and whatever foods devoured in their normal state. Essentially, this diet will comprise foods that might be eaten normally or prepared in a very way that is extremely basic, when every one of our precursors didn't have electric ovens, microwaves, or elective popular gadgets to arrange their food. Thus, this diet is designed according to that kind of way of life. You won't wander out chasing your food, choosing your vegetables, or running from wild creatures. Anyway, you'll make essential picks of foods that are generally regular and entirety. It expects that we tend to are organically fit to eating the way these antiquated progenitors of our own did. They ate the foods that were promptly accessible, high in healthful worth, contemporary, and indeed, bereft of added substances or preparing.

The foods they ate were high in protein, low in fat, awful fats, and contained all the fiber, nutrients, and minerals a sound body needs. Though simultaneously wiping out the terrible fats, sugars, and void calories (seared foods, candy, liquor, and refined grains) that have caused us, as a country, to be overweight and ridden with constant infection. The Paleo diet evades many of the foods we grew up reasoning about a fundamental piece of a sound diet - foods like grains (bread, oats, wafers, tortillas, and pasta) and dairy items (milk, cheeses, yogurt, frozen yogurt). In any case, these are the foods that can bring about the chief weight acquire - they contain undeniable degrees of carbs, fats, and salt. Eating them in enormous amounts contributes not exclusively to acquire yet to other well-being dangers, for example, diabetes and hypertension. Numerous competitors have accepted the Paleo diet due to its weight on protein from lean meats, fish, and poultry. Adding the new vegetables and natural products adds extra protein and a wide range of various fundamental nutrients, minerals, and fiber. The fresher and greener the vegetables, the better. Green, verdant vegetables like broccoli, spinach, kale, and different greens contain fundamental minerals like potassium and magnesium that few Americans lack in their diets. Furthermore, on the off chance that you'll have the option to get natural vegetables, that is far superior. The Paleo diet incorporates foods that can be pursued or accumulated, very much as they have been for an extremely prolonged period.

Fish and meats will be pursued, for example, and mushrooms, seeds, vegetables, and eggs can be assembled. The diet bars foods and added substances that didn't appear to be in the primary human diet. It incorporates grains, vegetables, prepared oils, and dairy items. Maybe the chief unfamiliar substance in the vogue human diet is recommended drugs. Paleo will, in general, devour drugs in crises and, in any case, dispose of them from their regular diet. Paleo expects to imitate the conventional way of life from multiple perspectives than simply the diet, albeit the diet is the chief fundamental way. They walk shoeless to create more grounded feet; give their bodies masses of time to rest during both evening and day; pay stacks of time outside - anything they can expect of that will adjust their ways of life to that of an ancient caveman.

Benefits of Paleo Diet

The paleo diet can be characterized as a healthy diet that exclusively permits the utilization of characteristic foods like meat, vegetables, and solid fats like coconut oils, macadamia oils, olive oils, etc. It restricts the utilization of grains, grain-basically based food items, sugar, and any very handled food. Characteristic all the way. That is the way into the paleo diet. Style might want not to be forfeited. Flavors might be utilized, and there are a few magnificent paleo formula books accessible that will instruct you to prepare sound, anyway delectable dishes. The underlying benefit to the paleo diet can be a decreased danger of infection.

Most people are utilized to the current diet with additives, destructive added substances, and diverse fake fixings that cause a wide range of medical problems and weight. Changing to the paleo diet will kill a large portion of these issues. The subsequent benefit can be a deficiency of abundance fat. The paleo diet means to downsize the number of carbs you devour. It can keep your glucose levels stable and increment your insulin affectability. That recommends that your body will be extra fixed on consuming off fat and remaining fit. The decrease of irritation is the third advantage. A large number of people, wherever the planet, grumbles of everyday a throbbing painfulness. Their body harms, yet they are doing not handle why. The explanation is aggravation because of the utilization of undesirable foods. The cells are aroused from the food they ate. By changing to the paleo diet, you might be devouring an extremely solid diet. It will lessen all aggravation and increment your feeling of prosperity. The fourth benefit is expanded bulk. Since the paleo diet spins around the utilization of bountiful meat measures, you will get a pile of protein. It will help in muscle development and recovery if you communicate in standard exercise. There will be bountiful less muscle breakdown. A great deal of muscle you have, the extra calories you consume. It essentially implies that you'll be lean, match, and solid. A better mind and organs are the fifth benefit.

The 6th advantage is decreased propensity to encourage sensitivities. Stylish day foods contain fixings that raise people's affectability to allergens. By removing these foods, our capacity to encourage hypersensitivities is enormously decreased. The seventh benefit is expanded energy. At first, the diet might be almost no intense to follow, and you'll not feel savvy because your body is freeing itself from poisons gathered from past dietary patterns. The change in diet additionally will be troublesome. However, when you live through this mound, it very well may be smooth cruising all the methodology. You'll understand yourself loaded with life and overflowing with energy. The higher than seven reasons should be sufficient to direct you to give up the paleo diet an attempt. You won't ever think back, and most people on the paleo diet say that it is one in every one of the least difficult things they could do. The way that the Paleo framework remains getting utilized today ought to demonstrate how successful it's.

By separating a person's admission to the principal fundamental, Paleo devotees figure out how to eliminate the modern sugars that litter popular food and because weight acquire. Henceforth, it just is reasonable that they will begin to get thinner - even with not many exercise meetings. Indeed, exercises for Paleo supporters are generally confined to a short however incredible burst that will rapidly consume off energy without drawing out the distress. With everything taken into account, the Paleo diet is an unimaginably successful philosophy of getting thinner. Be that as it may, one in everything about high issues of people utilizing Paleo is the absence of flavor and determination in their food. As referenced, some books give tips and deceive to Paleo experts to cook tasty dishes while not wandering from the Paleo idea. Henceforth, individuals who need to endeavor out this weight reduction routine don't have anything frozen. This diet is low in sugar and sodium because an excess of salt in the body isn't solid. Stone age men didn't have a stack of sugar or sodium in their diet because fake sugars, sugar, and salt didn't exist the way they will today. There was no requirement for unnecessary added substances. It was all unsettling enduring. The Paleo diet is tied in with returning to the basics by eating meat, contemporary organic product, contemporary vegetables, and staying away from a wide range of prepared foods that weren't accessible inside the Paleolithic period. In case you're attempting to get thinner, this is frequently the diet for you. It can work with your thin down because you might be eating enough of the legitimate things that your body will handle on what to attempt to with it and how to appropriately technique it. In flip, you'll practice which can urge your body to utilize your protein to assemble muscle, consume fat and eventually get more fit. In contrast to different diets, you'll have the option to get joy from your food by browsing recipes imprinted in an incredibly paleo formula book.

Paleo formula books embrace an assortment of heavenly dishes, similar to breakfast dinners of omelet biscuits, wiener pan-fried food, and steak and eggs. There isn't any need to skip dinners as the paleo diet needs you to eat when you are ravenous. This way, snacks like paleo hummus, an unpracticed smoothie, and bacon-wrapped dates can be made in your kitchen. Some paleo formula books conjointly incorporate soups like buffalo stew, gazpacho, and paleo meat stew for a luxurious dinner. Furthermore, elective paleo formula books embrace a shift of substantial dishes that cowl hamburger, poultry, and other game meats. You decidedly won't feel like you are on a tight eating routine as you chew into pork cook with a Dijon coat or have a couple of bun-less burgers in the middle of breaks at work. Sides like paleo pesto, simmered asparagus, basil spinach, and broccoli supplement these huge protein dishes.

While well-being edges of the paleo diet to get more fit are a motivating force to bear this severe diet, the well-being benefits are empowering. Alongside weight reduction, these common foods are perceived to help settle circulatory strain and cholesterol to solid levels while expanding energy, an undertaking the body can't do when over-burden with handled foods and sugar. The unmistakable medical advantages of this particular diet are a more grounded resistant safeguard in warding off sickness and infection, subsequently wiping out numerous well-being chances that are hence broad nowadays. For regardless of reason, you decide to be on a tight eating routine that began millennia prior. The characteristic foods alone can have a crucial enhancement for your well-being and essentialness. Seeds, nuts, natural products, vegetables, eggs, fish, and meat are regular Paleo diet foods. Low-quality nourishments like cakes, confections, sugars and baked goods are excluded from this diet, just like a genuine clarification for metabolic condition. Handled foods, dairy products, grains, and vegetable oils are prohibited from this diet. Even though meat might be a significant portion of the Paleo diet, foods like bacon, pepperoni, pork hotdogs, chicken wings, and store item should be kept away from the following fat substance. Grain and wheat items, including oats, rice, and grain, ought to be kept away from totally.

Foods grown from the ground are a fundamental piece

of this diet. They make for a solid nibble in the middle of suppers, regarding the foods devoured by stone-age men, all horticultural items, just as gluten-free ones, are excluded during this diet. One of the principal advantages of this diet is that processing will balance out at last. It expands digestion, promoting weight reduction. Since the Paleo diet has high protein content, a ton of competitors follow this diet. The fundamental foods like fish, chicken, nuts and slender meat give fiber and energy to the competitors promoting muscle advancement and weight decrease. Casein and gluten are the main sources of hypersensitivities, and they are found in a few prepared foods. In any case, they are not a portion of the Paleo diet foods, and thus, any can use this diet without worrying about stricken by hypersensitive responses. The danger of getting weight-associated sicknesses like diabetes and heart infections is impressively brought down since the Paleo diet consolidates a high fiber and low starch content. This magnificent diet setup incredibly profits a huge load of people.

Apple and Banana Fritters

Preparation Time: 20 Minutes

Cooking Time: 10 Minutes

Servings: 2

Ingredients:

- one egg
- one tbsp. (15 milliliters) canola oil
- Half mug (75 gram) chopped banana
- Half mug (63 gram) chopped apple
- one mug (120 gram) whole wheat pastry flour
- one tbsp. (one-Half gram) sugar substitute
- one tbsp. (one four-gram) baking grains
- Half mug (120 milliliters) rice milk
- Half tsp. nutmegs

Instructions:

- Blend flour, sugar substitute, and baking grains. Mix the milk, egg, and oil. Add banana, apple, and nutmeg.
- Blend into dry ingredients, moving until just moistened. Drop by tablespoonfuls into the hot oil—Fry for two to five-minute on a side until golden toast. Shift on paper towels before serving.

Tasty Orange Smoothie

Preparation Time: 20 Minutes

Cooking Time: 10 Minutes

Servings: 2

Ingredients:

- two tbsp. (30 gram) toast sugar
- one tsp. vanilla
- one-Half mug (355 milliliters) buttermilk
- one-third mug (83 gram) orange juice concentrate
- two ice cubes

Instructions:

- In a blender dish, blend buttermilk, orange juice concentrate, toast sugar, and vanilla. Enclose and blend until smooth.
- With blender running, add ice cubes one at a time through an opening in the lid. Blend until smooth and frothy.

Healthy Cinnamon Apple Fry Egg

Preparation Time: 25 Minutes

Cooking Time: 15 Minutes

Servings: 4

Ingredients:

- one tbsp. (15 gram) toast sugar
- three eggs
- one tbsp. cream
- one tbsp. without salt butter, divided
- one apple, peeled and diced thin
- Half tsp. cinnamon
- one tbsp. sour cream

Instructions:

- Soften two tsp—butter in egg saucepan. Add apple, cinnamon, and toast sugar. Fry until tender. Set aside. Blend eggs and cream until fluffy; set aside. Clean egg saucepan. Soften left-over butter, add in egg batter.
- Prepare as you would for an omelet. When eggs are ready to flip, turn them, then add to the center of the eggs the sour cream and, on top of that, the apple batter. Transfer it onto a plate.

Amazing Easy Breakfast Strata

Preparation Time: 34 Minutes

Cooking Time: 12 Minutes

Servings: 3

Ingredients:

- two mugs (225 gram) ground Cheddar cheese
- ten oz. (280 gram) frozen chopped broccoli, thawed
- two tbsp. (28 gram) without salt butter, melted
- two tbsp. (16 gram) flour
- one lb. (455 gram) sausage
- eight eggs
- ten slices whole wheat bread, diced
- three mugs (710 gram) rice milk
- one tbsp. dry mustard
- two tsp. basil

Instructions:

- Toast sausage in a large dish and drain. Whisk eggs in a large pan. Blend in the leftover ingredients thoroughly.

- Fill a baking pan with the mixture and brush it with nonstick margarine spray. Freeze for eight hours or overnight after enclosing.
- Preheat the oven to 350 degrees F. 60–70 minutes, or before a knife inserted in the middle comes out clean.

Delicious Latkes

Preparation Time: 40 Minutes

Cooking Time: 20 Minutes

Servings: 2

Ingredients:

- one egg
- Half mug (60 gram) bread crumbs
- four potatoes
- one tbsp. finely chopped onion
- two tbsp. (28 milliliters) canola oil

Instructions:

- Peel and grate potatoes. Squeeze in a kitchen towel to remove excess moisture. Merge all ingredients. Warm-up oil in a heavy dish.
- Drop batter onto a hot dish in One-fourth-mug measures and flatten with a fork into pancakes. Prepare until toasted. Turnover and finish preparing.

Low Carb Baked Pancake

Preparation Time: 50 Minutes

Cooking Time: 14 Minutes

Servings: 3

Ingredients:

- four eggs, slightly beaten
- One-fourth mug (55 gram) without salt butter
- one-Half mugs (180 gram) whole wheat pastry flour
- one-Half mugs (35 milliliters) rice milk
- one mug (170 gram) diced strawberries

Instructions:

- Gradually add flour and milk to eggs. Soften butter in a saucepan. Add batter over melted butter. Prepare at 400-degree Fahrenheit for about half an hour. Serve with fresh diced strawberries.

Gluten-Free Creamed Mushroom Fry Egg

Preparation Time: 20 Minutes

Cooking Time: 10 Minutes

Servings: 2

Ingredients:

- one shallot, chopped
- Half mug (35 gram) chopped mushrooms
- one tbsp. (13 gram) lard or other fat divided
- one tbsp. (four-gram) chopped fresh parsley
- Salt and black pepper
- One-fourth tsp. paprika
- two eggs

Instructions:

- In your omelet saucepan, fry the shallot and mushrooms in half the lard (reserve left-over to prepare the omelet) until the mushrooms soften and change color.
- Blend in the parsley, table salt or common salt and pepper, paprika, and Coconut Sour Cream.

- Separate the mushroom batter to a plate and reserve.
- Wipe the saucepan. Now create your omelet in line with Egg Fry Egg, using the mushrooms for filling.

Low Carb Cranberry Orange Oat Bran Cereal

Preparation Time: 40 Minutes

Cooking Time: 10 Minutes

Servings: 3

Ingredients:

- one-third mug (33 gram) oat bran
- One-fourth mug (38 gram) dried cranberries
- Half mug (120 milliliters) water
- Half mug (120 milliliters) orange juice

Instructions:

- Mix ingredients in a microwave-safe pan and prepare according to oat bran package microwave directions. Serve immediately.

Tasty Chicken-and-Pear Salad

Preparation Time: 20 Minutes

Cooking Time: 0 Minutes

Servings: 3

Ingredients:

- eight mugs (440 gram) leaf lettuce
- two tbsp. (28 milliliters) cider acetic acid
- Salt and black pepper
- two tbsp. (17.two gram) capers, drained and chopped
- third-fourth lb. (340 gram) boneless, skinless chicken breast
- six tbsp. (90 milliliters) olive oil, divided
- Half mug (60 gram) coarsely chopped walnuts
- two scallions, thinly diced
- one pear, cored and diced

Instructions:

- Brush your chicken with a little olive oil and start it preparing in your electrical tabletop grill. (If you don't have one, fry it over moderate-high heat in a very bit additional of the oil.)

- While that's happening, flip your oven on to 350-degree Fahrenheit. Chop your walnuts, unfold them on a shallow baking tin, and slide them into the oven. Set a timer for eight minutes. Dice your scallions, including the crisp part of the green shoot.
- Core and dice your pear. Pile your lettuce into a massive salad pan and add on the rest of the olive oil. Toss-toss toss till everything's coated.
- Add the acetic acid and toss once more. Throw it on your cutting board and slice it up. Now style your lettuce and add a very little table salt or common salt and pepper. Toss-toss-toss again.
- Now pile it on four plates. Beat every salad with a quarter of the diced chicken, one / four of the pear, two tbsp. (15 gram) of walnuts, One-fourth of the scallions, and a tbsp. Of capers.
- Serve immediately!

Garlic Fried Potatoes

Preparation Time: 40 Minutes

Cooking Time: 15 Minutes

Servings: 2

Ingredients:

- one lb. (455 gram) red potatoes, diced
- one mug (235 milliliters) small chicken broth
- one tbsp. (15 milliliters) olive oil
- third-fourth tsp. crushed garlic

Instructions:

- Clean potatoes and chop into Half-inch (one-centimeter) cubes; do not peel. Warm-up chicken broth in a nonstick dish just big enough to hold the potatoes in one layer. Add potatoes, cover, and boil for 15 minutes.
- The chicken broth will evaporate. Add olive oil and garlic. Toss for 15 minutes over moderate heat. Add black pepper to taste.

Delicious Pasta and Bean Salad

Preparation Time: 55 Minutes

Cooking Time: 15 Minutes

Servings: 3

Ingredients:

- three tbsp. (45 milliliters) acetic acid
- One-fourth mug (60 milliliters) light corn syrup
- One-fourth mug (60 milliliters) olive oil
- ten oz. (280 gram) frozen green beans
- one mug (100 gram) chopped celery
- one mug (150 gram) chopped green bell pepper
- one mug (160 gram) thinly diced red onion
- one mug (182 gram) cooked navy beans
- two mugs (280 gram) cooked whole wheat pasta

Instructions:

- In a moderate saucepan, mix acetic acid and corn syrup. Carry to a full boil, remove from heat, and cool. Add oil.

- Prepare frozen beans according to directions; drain; cool. In a big pan, blend vegetables, navy beans, and pasta. Add acetic acid and oil batter over vegetables.
- Freeze 24 hours, moving infrequently.

Gluten-Free Bean and Tomato Curry

Preparation Time: 45 Minutes

Cooking Time: 20 Minutes

Servings: 4

Ingredients:

- Half tsp. chopped garlic
- four mugs (720 gram) canned no-table salt or common salt-added tomatoes
- two mugs (450 gram) kidney beans, drained and rinsed
- one tbsp. (15 milliliters) canola oil
- one tsp. Mustard seed
- one tsp. cumin seeds
- one mug (160 gram) onion, chopped
- one tbsp. (six gram) fresh ginger, peeled and chopped
- one tsp. (two gram) curry grains

Instructions:

- Warm the oil in a large pot over medium heat and fry the mustard and cumin seeds together before they pop.

- Mix-fry the onion, ginger, and garlic until they are finely colored. Toss in the onions, peppers, and curry grains. Cook for 15 minutes, or until the sauce is thick and saucy.

Easy to Cook Bean and Cheddar Cheese Pie

Preparation Time: 60 Minutes

Cooking Time: 20 Minutes

Servings: 2

Ingredients:

- eight oz. (225 gram) no-table salt or common salt-added tomato sauce
- Half mug (75 gram) chopped green bell pepper
- One-fourth mug (40 gram) chopped onion
- third-fourth mug (93 gram) flour
- one-Half mugs (175 gram) ground Cheddar cheese, divided
- one-Half tsp. baking grains
- one-third mug (80 milliliters) rice milk
- one egg, beaten
- two mugs (328 gram) cooked chickpeas, drained
- two mugs (200 gram) cooked kidney beans, drained

Instructions:

- Heat the oven to 375-degree Fahrenheit. Sprinkle a ten-inch (25-centimeter) pie plate with non-stick margarine spray.
- Merge flour, Half mug (58 gram), cheddar cheese, and baking grains in a moderate pan. Blend in milk and egg until blended.
- Layout over bottom and up sides of pie plate. Merge Half mug (58 gram) of the left-over cheddar cheese and the left-over ingredients; spoon into pie plate.
- Drizzle with left-over cheddar cheese. Prepare about 15 minutes or till edges are puffy and lightweight toast.
- Let stand five minutes before cutting.

Nutritional Analysis:

Calories: 260, Fat:21g, Carbohydrates: 18g, Sodium: 14mg, Protein: 2g, Net carbs: 2g

Low-Fat Broccoli Wild Rice Casserole

Preparation Time: 45 Minutes

Cooking Time: 10 Minutes

Servings: 3

Ingredients:

- one-Half mugs (240 gram) wild rice
- six mugs (420 gram) broccoli
- two mugs (484 gram) decreased- the cream of mushroom soup
- two mugs (225 gram), small fat Cheddar cheese, ground

Instructions:

- Warm-up oven to 325-degree Fahrenheit. Prepare wild rice according to package directions. Layer rice in the bottom of a casserole saucepan.
- Vaporize broccoli for 15 minutes and layer on top of rice. Merge soup and cheddar cheese and spread on top of broccoli. Prepare, uncovered, for 45 minutes.

Amazing Barley and Pine Nut Casserole

Preparation Time: 40 Minutes

Cooking Time: 15 Minutes

Servings: 2

Ingredients:

- One-fourth mug (25 gram) chopped scallions
- One-fourth tsp. black pepper, freshly ground
- three mugs (355 milliliters) small chicken broth, heated to boiling
- one mug (200 gram) pearl barley
- Half mug (70 gram) pine nuts, divided
- three tbsp. (42 gram) without salt butter, divided
- one mug (160 gram) chopped onion
- Half mug (30 gram) chopped fresh parsley

Instructions:

- Warm-up oven to 375-degree Fahrenheit. Rinse and drain barley. Toast pine nuts in one tbsp. Butter in a dish.

- Separate nuts with a slotted spoon and set aside. Add left-over butter to the dish with onion and barley, mix until toasted.
- Blend in nuts, parsley, scallions, and pepper. Spoon into a one-Half-quart casserole plate. Add hot broth over the casserole and blend well.
- Prepare uncovered for one hour and 15 minutes.

Spinach-Stuffed Tomatoes

Preparation Time: 35 Minutes

Cooking Time: 15 Minutes

Servings: 4

Ingredients:

- One-fourth mug (25 gram) Parmesan, minced
- One-eighth tsp. pepper
- ten oz. (280 gram) fresh spinach
- , four tomatoes
- , one mug (115 gram) part-skim mozzarella, divided
- One-fourth mug (40 gram) onion, finely chopped
- two tbsp. (eight gram) fresh parsley, chopped

Instructions:

- Warm-up oven to 350-degree Fahrenheit. Vaporize or microwave the spinach in a coated pan till softened but still slightly crispy. Shift well and squeeze dry. Put in a huge pan.
- Dice and hollow out centers of tomatoes, reserving the pulp. Separate seeds.

- Chop pulp finely and increase spinach. Add Half mug (sixty gram) mozzarella cheddar cheese, onion, Parmesan, and pepper to spinach batter and mix well.
- Spoon evenly into tomato shells. Drizzle with left-over mozzarella and parsley.
- Arrange in an eight-inch (20 centimeters) spherical glass or ceramic baking plate and prepare for six minutes or until heated through.

Easy to Cook Chicken Breasts Baked in Creamy Herb Sauce

Preparation Time: 35 Minutes

Cooking Time: 15 Minutes

Servings: 3

Ingredients:

- One-fourth tsp. garlic grains
- One-fourth tsp. coriander
- One-fourth tsp. parsley
- One-fourth tsp. thyme
- four boneless skinless chicken breasts
- , one mug (230 gram) plain yogurt
- One-fourth mug (60 gram) sour cream
- Half tsp. lime peel, minced
- Half tsp. oregano
- One-fourth tsp. celery seed
- three tbsp. (45 milliliters) lime juice

Instructions:

- Warm-up oven to 375-degree Fahrenheit.

- Sprinkle roasting saucepan with non-stick margarine spray, put chicken breasts in it, and put aside.
- Mix all alternative ingredients. Baste chicken breasts with batter and prepare for 15 minutes.
- Separate from oven. Turn chicken breasts, baste with sauce, and prepare 15 minutes longer till meat is tender. Switch off the oven.
- Enclose chicken with foil and let stand in oven for five minutes.
- Separate aluminum foil, arrange chicken breasts on the serving plate and serve right away hot with any left-over sauce.

Low-Fat Smoked Chicken Minestrone

Preparation Time: 40 Minutes

Cooking Time: 20 Minutes

Servings: 4

Ingredients:

- One-fourth mug (40 gram) chopped onion
- one-third mug (43 gram) diced carrot
- one mug (113 gram) diced zucchini
- Half tsp. garlic grains
- Half lb. (225 gram) dry cannellini beans
- Half lb. (225 gram) dry chickpeas
- two smoked chicken thighs
- two mugs (475 milliliters), small chicken broth
- one tsp. basil
- one tsp. oregano
- two mugs (480 gram) no-table salt or common salt-added canned tomatoes

Instructions:

- Rinse beans and drain. Cook chicken in broth and enough water to cover until meat separates from bones. Chill, skim off the fat and remove meat from bones.

- Return meat to broth. Add other ingredients and boil one to one-Half hours until beans are tender. Add further water as needed.
- Garnish with Parmesan cheddar cheese.

Salmon Hash

Preparation Time: 55 Minutes

Cooking Time: 15 Minutes

Servings: 3

Ingredients:

- Half mug (75 gram) red bell peppers, chopped
- One-eighth tsp. pepper
- one clove garlic, crushed
- one tbsp. (15 milliliters) margarine
- Half mug (80 gram) chopped onion
- Half mug (75 gram) green bell peppers, chopped
- two moderate potatoes, diced and cooked
- one six oz. (455 gram) salmon

Instructions:

- Warm-up oil in one Q-inch (25 centimeters) non-stick dish over moderate-high heat. Fry onion, bell peppers, pepper, and garlic in oil.
- Blend in potatoes and salmon. Prepare uncovered, frequently moving, until hot.

Spicy Tasty Chicken Breasts

Preparation Time: 40 Minutes

Cooking Time: 15 Minutes

Servings: 2

Ingredients:

- One-fourth mug (60 milliliters) small- chicken broth
- one tsp. Worcestershire sauce
- one tbsp. (15 milliliters) lemon juice
- four chicken breasts

Instructions:

- Merge broth, Worcestershire sauce, and lemon juice. Inject into chicken breasts. Grill over moderate heat until done, about 15 minutes.

Paleo French Chicken

Preparation Time: 30 Minutes

Cooking Time: 15 Minutes

Servings: 2

Ingredients:

- one tbsp. (33 gram) mustard, coarse grain
- three tbsp. (45 milliliters) vermouth
- three tbsp. (45 milliliters) water
- one tbsp. (21 gram) without salt butter
- one tbsp. (15 milliliters) olive oil
- two boneless skinless chicken breasts
- one tbsp. (33 gram) honey mustard
- two tbsp. (30 milliliters) heavy cream

Instructions:

- Soften the butter in an exceedingly heavy-bottomed casserole. Add the oil. Toast the chicken on both sides, concerning a pair of to five minutes every facet.
- Carefully add off any excess fat. Add the mustards, vermouth, and water.

- Carry the liquid to a boil, scraping up the toast bits in the bottom of the saucepan.
- Enclose and boil for five minutes.
- Test the chicken to form certain it is done. Separate the meat into individual dishes and cover to stay heat.
- Add the cream and blend well.
- Serve the sauce over the chicken.

Low Carb Southwestern Skillet Supper

Preparation Time: 40 Minutes

Cooking Time: 15 Minutes

Servings: 3

Ingredients:

- Half tsp. cumin
- Half tsp. oregano
- Half mug (120 milliliters) chicken broth
- one lb. (455 gram) boneless skinless chicken breasts
- two tbsp. (30 milliliters) olive oil
- one mug (160 gram) onion, chopped
- two tsp. chili grains
- one-Half mugs (355 milliliters) small- V8 juice
- 19 oz. (532 gram) kidney beans

Instructions:

- Chop the chicken into 1h-inch (one centimeter) pieces.
- In hot oil, prepare chicken, onion, chili grains, cumin, and oregano until the chicken turns white.

- Blend in broth and juice.
- Warm-up until boiling, and then reduce heat to small.
- Cook five minutes. Add beans, liquid, and all, mix, cover, and boil for another five minutes. Blend infrequently.

Mexican Chicken Pasta Salad

Preparation Time: 60 Minutes

Cooking Time: 15 Minutes

Servings: 3

Ingredients:

- two tbsp. (30 milliliters) lemon juice
- four oz. (half gram) rigatoni
- one tbsp. olive oil
- one mug (150 gram) red bell peppers,
- two quarts water
- Half mug (120 milliliters) dry white wine
- four boneless skinless chicken breasts
- four cloves' garlic
- three tbsp. fresh basil, thinly diced
- One-eighth tsp. pepper
- two tbsp. (13 gram) ripe olives, thinly diced

Instructions:

- Carry water to a boil in moderate sauce saucepan.
- Add wine, chicken, and garlic. Decrease heat and boil fifteen minutes. Or till chicken is finished.

- Separate chicken and garlic from broth, reserving broth. Let chicken cool. Set aside. Crush garlic in an exceedingly small pan; add basil, pepper, and lemon juice. Merge well and put aside.
- Carry reserved broth to a boil. Add pasta. Prepare 12 minutes or until al dente. Shift. Rinse beneath cold water. Shift.
- Toss pasta with olive oil. Mix reserved garlic-lemon batter, chicken, pasta, bell peppers, and olives in a huge pan. Toss gently.
- Chill at least one hour.

Marinated Flank Steak

Preparation Time: 55 Minutes

Cooking Time: 20 Minutes

Servings: 3

Ingredients:

- one tsp. dried rosemary
- one tbsp. (15 milliliters) chipotle Chile canned in adobo, chopped
- One-fourth mug (60 milliliters) water
- three lb. flank steak
- one papaya wedge, one-inch wide
- one tbsp. (seven gram) smoked paprika
- two garlic cloves, peeled
- one tsp. honey
- two tbsp. (26 gram) lard or other fat

Instructions:

- Use a knife with a very sharp, thin blade to lightly score the surface of your steak in squares or diamonds concerning two inches (five centimeter) apart.

- Place it during a big zipper-lock bag. Place everything else in the food processor.
- Don't take away the skin from the papaya; it's the richest supply of papain, the tenderizing enzyme. Run the processor until you have got a purée. Add it into the bag with the steak and seal it up, pressing the air out as you go. Turn the bag many times to coat.
- Throw the bag with the steak into the fridge and let it marinate for an hour or so—the papaya is a powerful tenderizer and don't let it go too long.
- The 1st time I used the papaya, I wound up with a mushy steak! When it's time to prepare, put your massive, significant dish over highest heat and let it get sensible and hot. Soften the lard and slosh it around.
- Now pull your steak out of the marinade and throw it in the dish—watch out, it will spit! Pan-broil it quickly until seared on both sides but still pink within the center. Time will depend on the thickness of your steak; however, it shouldn't take additional than three to 15 minutes per aspect.
- Separate to a platter and slice skinny across the grain to serve right away.

Asian-old Shredded Beef Stew

Preparation Time: 55 Minutes

Cooking Time: 25 Minutes

Servings: 3

Ingredients:

- Half green bell peppers
- two jalapeño peppers
- two tbsp. (26 gram) lard
- four garlic cloves, crushed
- two tsp. ground cumin
- one-Half lb. (710 gram) beef round
- Half big onion, chopped, plus one moderate onion, diced thin
- one big carrot, peeled and diced
- one bay leaf
- one mug (235 milliliters) beef broth
- Half red bell peppers
- Half yellow bell peppers
- Salt and black pepper

Instructions:

- Chop your beef into one-in. cubes. In your huge, serious dish, over moderate-high heat, soften the lard or coconut oil and start browning the meat cubes. Don't crowd them; higher to do a try of batches.

- While the beef is browning, peel your onion and chop it into one-in. (a try of. Five centimeter) chunks.

- Peel the daikon and carrot and slice diagonally, regarding One-fourth-in. (half dozen mm) thick. Up by the thick finish of each, you'll get huge slices, in fact, therefore halve or quarter them to induce stuff in equally, sized items.

- Put of these vegetables, and also the mushrooms, in your slow cooker.

- By the suggests that, keep in mind to turn your beef cubes whereas you're cutting all that stuff up! Using a pointy knife, slice the gingerroot as thinly as doable, across the grain. Peel the garlic and slice it paper thin, too.

- Add these to the vegetables and combine them in.

- Throw within the star anise, too. Your beef chunks ought to be nicely toasted now.
- Put them on high of the vegetables among the slow cooker.
- Currently combine the meat broth, coconut amines, honey, and pepper.
- Add it over everything, cowl the pot, set it to tiny, and forget about it for eight to ten hours serve right away.

Crispy Beef Soft Tacos

Preparation Time: 45 Minutes

Cooking Time: 20 Minutes

Servings: 3

Ingredients:

- Half red onion, diced
- one avocado, diced
- one moderate tomato, diced
- Crispy Shredded Beef (opposite)
- Coconut Sour Cream
- two mugs (110 gram) ground lettuce, iceberg or romaine

Instructions:

- A lot of this stuff can and should be made in advance—the Eggy Wraps, the Crispy Shredded Beef, the Coconut Sour Cream, and possibly the Salsa.
- Warm the beef; dice the onion, avocado, and tomato; and shred the lettuce. Now just set everything out and let people build their soft tacos!

Asian-Style Beans

Preparation Time: 65 Minutes

Cooking Time: 20 Minutes

Servings: 2

Ingredients:

- eight oz. (225 gram) dried kidney beans
- six mugs water
- two tbsp. (30 milliliters) acetic acid
- Half tsp. garlic grains
- one tsp. (three gram) onion grains
- one tbsp. chili grains

Instructions:

- Rinse the beans and place them in a large pot with enough water to cover them. Bring to a boil and cook for two minutes. Remove from the sun and set aside for an hour.
- Return to a high fire, add the acetic acid, garlic, onion, and chilly grains, and cook for one to half-hours, or until the beans are tender. If the beans get too dry, add some water or a low- chicken broth.

Beef Kabobs

Preparation Time: 60 Minutes

Cooking Time: 20 Minutes

Servings: 3

Ingredients:

- One-fourth mug (60 milliliters) olive oil
- One-fourth mug (60 milliliters) lemon juice
- two tbsp. (30 milliliters) Worcestershire sauce
- Half tsp. chopped garlic
- one tsp. (two gram) coarsely ground black pepper
- one lb. (455 gram) beef round steak, chop in one-inch cubes
- two mugs (140 gram) mushrooms

Instructions:

- Merge all ingredients except beef and mushrooms. Add beef cubes. Enclose and freeze overnight, turning meat infrequently. Thread meat and mushrooms on skewers. Grill over fire to desired doneness, turning often.

Nutritional Analysis:

Calories: 250, Fat:19g, Carbohydrates: 21g, Sodium: 21mg, Protein: 2g, Net carbs: 2g

Low Carb Paleo Ground Beef Stroganoff

Preparation Time: 55 Minutes

Cooking Time: 15 Minutes

Servings: 2

Ingredients:

- one third-fourth mugs (414 milliliters) water
- eight oz. (225 gram) whole wheat noodles, cooked and drained
- eight tbsp. (120 gram) plain fat-free yogurt
- Half lb. (225 gram) ground beef, extra lean
- Half mug (35 gram) diced mushrooms
- one packet onion soup blend
- one tbsp. whole wheat flour

Instructions:

- Toast beef and drain. Add mushrooms. Whisk dry soup blend and flour into water and heat. Blend until condensed.
- Mix condensed onion soup and cooked beef. Serve over whole wheat noodles. Garnish with a dollop of yogurt.

Skillet Pork Chops

Preparation Time: 45 Minutes

Cooking Time: 15 Minutes

Servings: 4

Ingredients:

- Half mug (120 milliliters) small chicken broth
- Half mug (120 milliliters) barbecue sauce
- four mugs (900 gram) no-table salt or common salt-added canned pinto beans, drained
- two jalapeno peppers, chopped
- six pork loin chops
- one tbsp. (15 milliliters) olive oil
- one mug (160 gram) onion, chopped
- Half tsp. chopped garlic

Instructions:

- In a big dish, sear pork chops in oil for 15 minutes, or until toast. Separate pork chops and put on a plate.
- Add onion and garlic to dish; prepare ten minutes. Blend in broth, barbecue sauce, beans, and jalapenos.

- Warm-up batter to a boil. Return pork to dish. Decrease heat; cover and boil 50 to one hour, move sauce, and turn chops infrequently until meat is fork-tender.

Tasty Pork and Apple Curry

Preparation Time: 60 Minutes

Cooking Time: 20 Minutes

Servings: 3

Ingredients:

- one apple, peeled and diced
- Half mug (75 gram) red bell pepper, chop in strips
- Half mug (120 milliliters) small chicken broth
- one tsp. (two gram) corn-starch
- two tbsp. (30 milliliters) olive oil
- four pork loin chops
- Half mug (80 gram) onion, thinly diced
- One-fourth tsp. chopped garlic
- Half tsp. cinnamon
- One-fourth tsp. freshly ground black pepper

Instructions:

- In a heavy frying saucepan, heat oil over moderate-high heat.

- Prepare pork chops until toasted on both sides and virtually cooked through; take away from saucepan and set aside.
- Over moderate heat, prepare the onion, garlic, apple, and red bell pepper strips for two minutes or until softened.
- Blend chicken broth with corn-starch; raise saucepan together with curry grains, cumin, and cinnamon; prepare for one or a pair of minutes, or till slightly decreased and condensed. Return pork chops to frying saucepan.
- Prepare for one or two minutes or till heated through. Serve pork chops with sauce and drizzle with pepper.

Delicious Blend-Fried Pork and Cabbage

Preparation Time: 30 Minutes

Cooking Time: 15 Minutes

Servings: 3

Ingredients:

- one mug (150 gram) apple, diced thinly
- three tbsp. (45 milliliters) honey
- one lb. (455 gram) pork loin chops, diced thinly
- one tbsp. (15 milliliters) olive oil
- four mugs (280 gram) cabbage, ground

Instructions:

- Dice pork. Warm-up oil in wok or dish, add pork and mix-fry until no longer pink, about 15 minutes. Add apples and honey, mix-fry one minute. Add cabbage and mix-fry for 30 to 45 seconds, or until heated through, but still crispy.

Delightful Texas Style Steak

Preparation Time: 55 Minutes

Cooking Time: 20 Minutes

Servings: 3

Ingredients:

- Half mug (75 gram) green peppers, chopped
- Half mug (80 gram) onions, chopped
- one mug (235 milliliters) fat-free beef broth
- Half mug (120 milliliters) tomato juice
- Half mug (63 gram) flour
- two Half tsp. chili grains, divided
- one-Half lb. (680 gram) beef round steak
- two tbsp. (30 milliliters) margarine
- One-fourth tsp. garlic grains
- One-fourth tsp. ground cumin

Instructions:

- Blend flour, table salt or common salt, and one-Half tsp. (four gram) chili grains well and put in pie saucepan. Dredge meat in the flour batter. Place oil in a very serious frying saucepan and warmth over moderate heat.

- Add meat and toast on both sides. Transfer steaks to a one and hour quart casserole. Fry peppers and onions over moderate heat within the saucepan in that the meat was toasted, moving frequently. Separate vegetables with a slotted spoon and spread over meat. Add out any left-over fat. Add beef broth to frying saucepan and prepare and combine over moderate heat to soak up and toast particles left-over in the saucepan.
- Add left-over ingredients to broth. Merge well and add over meat. Blend the meat and vegetables gently with a fork to distribute the broth and vegetables. Enclose tightly and prepare at 325-degree Fahrenheit for about one-one and half hour hours or until the meat is tender.

Tasty Cinnamon Apple Pork Tenderloin

Preparation Time: 60 Minutes

Cooking Time: 15 Minutes

Servings: 3

Ingredients:

- one lb. (455 gram) pork tenderloin
- two tbsp. (16 gram) corn-starch
- one tsp. ground cinnamon
- two apples, peeled, cored, diced
- two tbsp. (one eight gram) raisins

Instructions:

- Warm-up the oven to 400-degree Fahrenheit. Put the pork tenderloin in a roasting saucepan or casserole plate with a lid. Mix the left-over ingredients in a pan and mix. Spoon the apple batter around the pork tenderloin.
- Enclose and prepare 40 minutes. Separate the lid and spoon the apple batter over the tenderloin. Return to the oven and prepare 15 minutes longer until tenderloin is toasted and cooked through.

Delightful Apple Pork Roast

Preparation Time: 55 Minutes

Cooking Time: 15 Minutes

Servings: 3

Ingredients:

- eight small onions, peeled but left whole
- two tbsp. (16 gram) flour
- four lb. pork loin roast
- third-fourth tsp. pepper
- eight apples, cored
- two Half mugs (570 milliliters) apple cider

Instructions:

- Drizzle pepper over pork roast and put in roasting saucepan. Roast at 325-degree Fahrenheit for one and half hour hours. Add off fat.
- Put onions and apples in alternate positions around roast. Add one and half hour mugs cider and roast a more one and half hour hours, basting typically.

- Skim off fat when done. Add flour and left-over cider to saucepan liquid. Prepare batter till smooth and condensed, moving frequently. Put roast on platter and add sauce over to serve straight away.

Low-Fat Greek Islands Fish

Preparation Time: 50 Minutes

Cooking Time: 20 Minutes

Servings: 3

Ingredients:

- Half mug artichoke hearts, chopped
- Half mug ripe olives, chopped
- six tilapia fillets
- one mug no table salt or common salt added tomatoes, diced

Instructions:

- Put fillets in a baking saucepan coated with non-stick preparing spray. Beat with left-over ingredients. Prepare at 400-degree Fahrenheit for 15 minutes or until fish flakes easily.

Crave Special Bean and Corn Burritos

Preparation Time: 50 Minutes

Cooking Time: 20 Minutes

Servings: 4

Ingredients:

- Half tsp. chopped garlic
- one tsp. ground cumin
- One-eighth tsp. white pepper
- two mugs (200 gram) cooked kidney beans, drained and mashed
- Half mug (80 gram) chopped onion
- One-fourth mug (38 gram) diced green bell pepper
- one tsp. chopped jalapeño pepper
- one mug (260 gram) salsa
- One-fourth mug (60 gram) fat-free sour cream
- One-fourth mug chopped fresh cilantro

Instructions:

- Sprinkle a non-stick dish with non-stick margarine spray. Put over moderate heat till hot. Add onion, bell pepper, jalapeño, and garlic. Fry till tender. Blend in cumin and white pepper. Prepare one minute, moving constantly.

- Separate from heat; combine in mashed beans and corn. Layout Half mug (50 gram) bean batter evenly over surface of each tortilla. Drizzle three tbsp. cheddar cheese down center of each tortilla.
- Roll up tortillas and put seam aspect down on a baking sheet. Prepare at 425-degree Fahrenheit (220°C, gas mark seven) for seven to eight minutes or until completely heated. For every serving, prime each burrito with One-fourth mug (65 gram) salsa and one tbsp. sour cream. Garnish with recent cilantro.

Delicious Asian Rice

Preparation Time: 45 Minutes

Cooking Time: 20 Minutes

Servings: 3

Ingredients:

- one mug (220 gram) cooked toast rice
- two tbsp. (28 milliliters) olive oil
- Half mug (80 gram) chopped onion
- One-fourth lb. (113 gram) ground Cheddar cheese
- one jalapeño pepper, chopped

Instructions:

- Toast rice in oil. Add left-over ingredients. Enclose and boil until heated through and cheddar cheese is melted. Serve right away.

Asian Beef Salad

Preparation Time: 55 Minutes

Cooking Time: 25 Minutes

Servings: 3

Ingredients:

- Half tsp. cumin
- one mug (100 gram) cooked kidney beans, drained and rinsed
- one lb. (455 gram) chickpeas, drained and rinsed
- one mug (180 gram) diced tomato
- one lb. (455 gram) ground beef, extra lean
- Half mug (80 gram) chopped onion
- one tbsp. chili grains
- two tsp. oregano
- two mugs (110 gram) iceberg lettuce
- Half mug (58 gram) ground Cheddar cheese

Instructions:

- Prepare ground beef and onion in a dish over moderate-high heat until beef is no longer pink, ten to 12 minutes. Shift. Blend in chili grains, oregano, and cumin. Prepare for one minute. Merge in beans, chickpeas, and tomato.

- Portion lettuce onto serving plates. Beat with ground cheddar cheese. Then top with beef batter.

Gluten-Free Spinach Balls

Preparation Time: 30 Minutes

Cooking Time: 15 Minutes

Servings: 2

Ingredients:

- Half mug (50 gram) minced Parmesan cheddar cheese
- three eggs, beaten
- ten oz. (280 gram) frozen spinach, thawed and drained
- one mug (72 gram) stuffing blend, crushed
- One-fourth mug (55 gram) without salt butter, softened
- One-eighth tsp. nutmeg

Instructions:

- Put spinach on paper towels and squeeze until barely moist. Mix spinach and next five ingredients in a pan. Merge well.
- Shape into two Half-inch (six-centimeter) balls with an ice cream scoop. Put on waxed paper–lined baking sheet.

- Enclose and freeze eight hours. Prepare spinach balls on a baking sheet coated with non-stick margarine spray and prepare at 350-degree Fahrenheit for 15 minutes until hot. Shift on paper towels.

Vegetable Cloak

Preparation Time: 35 Minutes

Cooking Time: 10 Minutes

Servings: 3

Ingredients:

- four oz. (115 gram) mushrooms, chopped
- One-fourth mug (25 gram) chopped scallions
- Half tsp. chopped garlic
- one mug (119 gram) diced cucumber
- one mug (113 gram) diced zucchini
- Half mug (65 gram) diced carrot
- three oz. (85 gram) cream cheddar cheese
- four whole wheat tortillas
- One-fourth mug (65 gram) salsa

Instructions:

- Mix all vegetables. Layout cream cheddar cheese on tortilla. Layout vegetables and salsa over cream cheddar cheese. Roll up. Serve right away.

Delightful Pecan-Stuffed Mushrooms

Preparation Time: 55 Minutes

Cooking Time: 20 Minutes

Servings: 2

Ingredients:

- 12 big mushrooms
- two tbsp. (20 gram) chopped onion
- two tbsp. (28 gram) without salt butter
- Half mug (55 gram) chopped pecans
- Half mug (60 gram) whole wheat bread crumbs
- one tsp. lemon juice

Instructions:

- Clean mushrooms gently in cool water or wipe with damp cloth. Separate and chop stems. Fry onion in butter; add chopped stems, pecans, bread crumbs, and lemon juice. Merge well. Mound mushroom caps with stuffing.
- Broil four minutes about four inches (ten centimeter) from heat or prepare in microwave oven on 100 percent power two to five minutes until heated through.

Gluten-Free Green Beans and Tomatoes

Preparation Time: 60 Minutes

Cooking Time: 20 Minutes

Servings: 3

Ingredients:

- One-fourth mug (40 gram) onion, chopped
- one mug (180 gram) tomatoes, chopped
- Half lb. (225 gram) green beans
- one tbsp. (15 millilitres) olive oil
- One-fourth mug (38 gram) red bell pepper, chopped
- Half tsp. dried rosemary

Instructions:

- Prepare green beans in boiling water until tender. Shift and set aside. In a dish, heat oil and fry red bell pepper and onion until soft. Add tomatoes, basil, and rosemary. Blend in green beans and heat through.

Low Carb Hot and Garlicky Brussels Sprouts

Preparation Time: 50 Minutes

Cooking Time: 20 Minutes

Servings: 3

Ingredients:

- two garlic cloves, chopped
- One-fourth tsp. red-pepper flakes
- one lb. (455 gram) brussels sprouts
- two tbsp. (26 gram) bacon grease or lard
- Salt to taste

Instructions:

- Cut your brussels sprouts and halve them. Vaporize them for simply a few minutes in the microwave or on the stovetop. Shift and pat dry. Put your big, significant dish over high heat. Add the bacon grease and let it get smart and hot.
- Add your Brussels, watching out for spitting oil! (The better you dry your Brussels, the less spitting there will be.)

- Let them fry without moving for a moment, then flip and repeat-keep going till they are toasted and tender.
- Now mix within the garlic and red pepper, and provide them simply another minute or two, moving constantly. Salt, if you want.

The Simplest Eggplant

Preparation Time: 30 Minutes

Cooking Time: 15 Minutes

Servings: 3

Ingredients:

- one eggplant
- Olive oil—a lot of olive oil. I mean a whole lot of olive oil.

Instructions:

- Dice your eggplant crosswise into rounds about one-third in. (eight mm) thick. Put your huge, heavy dish over moderate-high heat and add One-fourth in olive oil (six mm).
- Get it smart and hot. Now fry your eggplant slices, three or four at a time, till they're golden toast on each side.
- They can suck up olive oil like faculty students on spring break suck down beer, thus be ready to add additional as required.

- When your eggplant is fantastically golden on each side, serve instantly hot, with table salt or common salt and pepper. That is all. I served the first slices, whereas subsequent batches were still frying because the hot-and crisp issue is half of the appeal.

Delicious Caramel Corn

Preparation Time: 35 Minutes

Cooking Time: 15 Minutes

Servings: 3

Ingredients:

- One-fourth mug (60 millilitres) corn syrup
- Half tsp. baking soda
- four quarts (128 gram) popped popcorn
- Half mug (half a gram) without salt butter
- one mug (225 gram) toast sugar
- two mugs (290 gram) peanuts

Instructions:

- Prepare butter, toast, sugar, and syrup for one-Half minutes; mix and prepare for a further two to five minutes until a rolling boil. Take off heat and add soda. Blend well. Add batter over popped corn and nuts in a grocery bag and shake.
- Microwave one minute, shake; one minute, shake; 30 seconds, shake; 30 seconds, shake. Add into a saucepan, cool, and eat.

Amazing Roasted Mexican Vegetable

Preparation Time: 50 Minutes

Cooking Time: 15 Minutes

Servings: 3

Ingredients:

- Half mug (75 gram) green bell pepper,
- two tbsp. (30 millilitres) olive oil
- Half tsp. chopped garlic
- Half tsp. dried basil
- Half tsp. dried oregano
- Half mug (80 gram) onion, diced into wedges
- One-fourth mug (45 gram) plum tomato halves
- Half mug (56 gram) zucchini, chop in one-inch slices
- Half mug (35 gram) mushrooms, chop in half

Instructions:

- Warm-up oven to 400-degree Fahrenheit. Mix oil, garlic, basil, and oregano in a resealable plastic bag. Add onion, green bell pepper, tomatoes, zucchini, and mushrooms, and shake to coat evenly.

- Cover a) roasting saucepan with non-stick margarine spray. Put the vegetables in a single layer in the saucepan. Roast for 15 minutes or until crisp.

Gluten-Free Green Beans with Caramelized Pearl Onions

Preparation Time: 50 Minutes

Cooking Time: 20 Minutes

Servings: 4

Ingredients:

- one-third mug (75 gram) without salt butter
- two lb. (910 gram) fresh green beans
- one lb. (455 gram) pearl onions
- Half mug (115 gram) toast sugar

Instructions:

- Arrange beans in a very steamer basket over boiling water. Enclose and steam fifteen minutes; put aside.
- Put onions in boiling water for three minutes. Shift and rinse with cold water. Chop off root ends of onions and peel.
- Arrange onions in steamer basket over boiling water. Enclose and steam fifteen minutes. Set onions aside. Soften butter in a serious dish over moderate heat.

- Add sugar, and prepare, constantly moving, till bubbly. Add onions; prepare three minutes, moving constantly.
- Add beans and prepare, constantly moving, until totally heated.

Oat Bran Peanut Cookies

Preparation Time: 40 Minutes

Cooking Time: 15 Minutes

Servings: 2

Ingredients:

- Half mug (115 gram) packed toast sugar
- Half mug (100 gram) sugar
- two mugs (200 gram) oat bran
- one mug (125 gram) flour
- Half mug (120 millilitres) canola oil
- one mug (260 gram) decreased- peanut butter
- two eggs
- one tsp. baking grains
- one tsp. baking soda

Instructions:

- Warm-up oven to 350-degree Fahrenheit. In a big pan, blend the oil, peanut butter, and eggs until well blended.
- Merge in the toasted sugar, then the left-over ingredients.

- Freeze overnight. Form into one-inch balls and put on a not-greased baking sheet. Press down on the tops of the cookies with a fork to form the typical crisscross pattern.
- Prepare for 15 minutes, or until lightly toasted.

Low Carb Red and Blue Berry Cobbler

Preparation Time: 45 Minutes

Cooking Time: 15 Minutes

Servings: 4

Ingredients:

- one mug (125 gram) flour
- two tbsp. (26 gram) plus Half tsp. (two gram) sugar divided
- two tsp. baking grains
- two tbsp. (28 gram) without salt butter,
- two mugs' strawberries, halved
- two mugs (290 gram) blueberries
- Half mug (120 millilitres) raspberry jam
- two tbsp. (eight gram) corn-starch
- two tbsp. (30 millilitres) rice milk
- one egg

Instructions:

- Warm-up oven to 425-degree Fahrenheit. Grease a one-Half-quart baking plate. In a huge pan, blend berries, jam, and corn starch. Merge gently. Layout in the prepared baking plate.

Prepare for 15 to fifteen minutes, or until berries begin to bubble. Meanwhile, during a massive pan, blend flour, two tbsp. (26 gram) sugar, and baking grains. Merge well. With a pastry blender or two forks, chop in butter till crumbly.

- During a small pan, mix milk and egg; whisk well. Mix into flour batter till stiff dough forms, adding additional milk if necessary. On a gently floured surface, roll out dough to Half-in. Thickness.
- With a cookie cutter, chop out stars or different shapes. Blend hot fruit chunks batter; high with dough chop-outs. Drizzle chop-outs with left-over Half tsp. (a pair of grams) sugar. Prepare for ten to fifteen minutes, or until fruit chunks bubbles around edges and biscuits are light-weight golden Toast

Low Carb Dark Chocolate Frozen Custard

Preparation Time: 45 Minutes

Cooking Time: 20 Minutes

Servings: 4

Ingredients:

- One-fourth mug (85 gram) honey
- One-fourth tsp. French vanilla liquid stevia
- One-fourth tsp. chocolate liquid stevia
- 27 fluid oz. (793 millilitres) without sweet coconut milk
- four oz. (115 gram) bitter chocolate
- six egg yolks

Instructions:

- A huge, significant-bottomed saucepan, over very tiny heat, slowly heat the coconut milk with the chocolate. Whisk sometimes as the chocolate melts because it takes a little bit of whisking to incorporate the chocolate into the coconut milk.
- When the coconut milk is heat and the chocolate melted, whisk the honey and liquid stevia. Keep heating. Separate your yolks into a moderate-

size pan and whisk them up. When the coconut milk/chocolate batter is just below a boil, use a spoon to transfer regarding Half mug (a hundred and twenty millilitres); (that's what my ladle holds) into the pan of egg yolks and immediately whisk very well. Transfer another ladleful into the yolks, and once more, whisk very well.

- Now add this batter into the main pot of coconut milk, whisking all the whereas. Prepare a touch longer, letting the batter thicken up a small amount. Switch off the burner, let it cool, then stick it in the fridge and chill it well. When dessert time rolls around, transfer your chilled custard to your ice cream freezer and freeze in step with the directions that return along with your unit. Serve—if you can bear to share it.

NOTE

CPSIA information can be obtained
at www.ICGtesting.com
Printed in the USA
BVHW012055100721
611638BV00008B/121